In Our Shoes

Experiences of children and young people in the Family Justice System

Curated by Dawn Reeves

First edition published in Great Britain in 2021 by Shared Press

Published by Shared Press
www.sharedpress.co.uk

Copyright © Cafcass 2021

The right of Cafcass has been asserted in accordance with the Copyright, Designs and Patents Act 1988.

A catalogue record for this book is available from the British Library.

All rights reserved. No part of this publication may be reproduced, transmitted, or stored in a retrieval system in any form or by any means without the prior written permission of the publisher.

Editing by Victoria Robson
Design and typesetting by James Warren

Shared Press' policy is to use papers that are natural, renewable, recyclable products from well-managed forests in accordance with the rules of the Forest Stewardship Council.

Acknowledgements

On behalf of the Family Justice Young People's Board (FJYPB) we'd like to thank everyone who has contributed to the production of our book: our sponsors at Cafcass, particularly Jennifer Gibbon-Lynch, Luba Musa-Eiggie, Claire Evans, Marie Gittins and Jacky Tiotto.

Thanks to the team at Shared Press, Dawn Reeves, Alicia Fox, Iseabail Shaw Wraight, and Fran Collingham, to editor Victoria Robson and designer James Warren.

Contents

Foreword — 3
Jacky Tiotto – Chief Executive, Cafcass

Introduction — 5
The Family Justice Young People's Board

Chapter 1 — 9
Our experiences of family law proceedings

Chapter 2 — 29
Our experiences of family conflict

Chapter 3 — 51
Our diverse experiences

Chapter 4 — 73
Our experiences of health and well-being

Chapter 5 — 95
Our experiences of being understood and the difference this makes

Chapter 6 — 117
Next steps – postscript and resources

Foreword

'In my shoes' means many different things to many different people. I consider it to mean that you never really understand a person until you consider things from their point of view and stay a while with that experience.

This is why at Cafcass we value so deeply the work and experiences of our Family Justice Young People's Board (FJYPB). All members of the board (there are more than 70 aged between eight and 25 years old) have all had either direct experience of the family justice system or have an interest in children's rights and the family courts.

Their shoes are the ones we try to walk in to improve our work and to understand how we can continually improve their journey through court proceedings. By listening to their words, we feel their emotions; by talking with them, we get to know what feels hard on their journey and what makes it easier. Our absolute first responsibility is to be as accurate as we can in describing what their shoes feel like, to protect and promote their safety and welfare, and to give them hope for the future – to make their shoes more comfortable.

But the stories in this book are not comfortable. Children are asking us as professionals in the family justice system to listen better, then listen some more and don't assume that they understand everything. They want us to respect that information is power, power that they need and must have. They need to know what we are saying to the courts, and we need to tell them what we have told their families. We need to listen to understand rather than to reply.

You will be moved by this book – of that I have no doubt. But it's what you do with it that will count most and make their efforts here worthwhile. I would like to thank all the young people who have generously shared their experiences in such creative and compelling ways – and a special thanks for taking the time to do so during a global pandemic in which children have been the biggest losers.

The book is a unique opportunity for any professional working in the family justice system to understand what it's really like to walk in their shoes, to live their lives and to be able to influence them for the good. I know you will enjoy reading it as much as I have and I hope you can learn something from it. Your challenge now is what to do next so that the privilege of walking with them makes a difference to their young lives, now and tomorrow.

Jacky Tiotto
Chief Executive, Cafcass

Introduction – from us to you

Thank you for picking up this book. We hope it inspires and guides your work with children and young people in the family justice system.

Our collection of experiences and poems show the realities of life for children and young people in the family justice system: the challenges we've had to deal with, the twists and turns of sometimes mysterious processes, in some cases the joy of a resolution and the small moments that stay with us.

As members of the Family Justice Young People's Board, we've shared what we think and how we feel, what matters to us and our hopes for the future. It can be hard to talk about emotions to professionals in formal settings, so the opportunity to write about our experiences and help make sense of them is important. You'll read about our diversity as a group, and the different circumstances in which we've found ourselves. These are some of the situations we've lived through to become the people we are now.

It means a lot to us to know that we're playing a part in changing the way the system works, so that the experiences of other young people who come after us are better.

We hope these personal insights spark a connection. We'd like you to take a breath and reflect on how you develop your own work with the young people you've already met and are yet to meet. We hope it inspires you to think about the best approaches, make the best policies, and develop training to meet children's needs.

Although the book is designed for professionals working in this world, we hope that it might find its way to other children going through proceedings. We want them to find some comfort and support in knowing they are not alone, and that with help, things do get better. As well as messages for professionals, we've included some thoughts for other young people, the sorts of things we wished another young person had said to us in the eye of the storm.

Some 140,000 children experience the family justice system each year. They need your help, and you need to know how best to help them. We want the book to be a transformational tool and would love it if the book became something you come back to again and again.

Walk a while in our shoes and enjoy the read!

How to use this book
The book is divided into five chapters covering: family justice proceedings, family conflict, diversity, health and wellbeing, and being understood. Hearing our voices is the common thread throughout the book. Our final chapter is designed to help you make the most of what you've read. It's a practical section that signposts further information and support.

Trigger warning
Some of the pieces may be distressing to readers who have experienced abuse of different kinds or traumatic life events. The purpose of the book is to help professionals in the family justice system see our truths and do something about them. We've tried to share what's essential about those experiences and we acknowledge this can be tough to read.

In writing about our lives, we were supported by our trusted and professionally-trained FJYPB co-ordinator who explained the process, encouraged us and was there to pick up any issues. We have also been supported with creative writing workshops and sensitive editing that stays true to what we wanted to say. Members of the Board have also been involved in developing and choosing the design of the book.

Reflect and connect
Each chapter has a series of reflective questions raised by our experiences. We hope they help guide your thinking and encourage you to make connections between your experiences and ours. We might not always have much in common with the professionals we meet but we are an inquisitive bunch, always asking questions. We invite you to take the same approach – keep asking questions of yourself and your organisations to get to the heart of the matter, to spot what needs to change and prompt thinking about how you can move forward.

Importantly, we ask you to do this because, as you already know, the decisions that are made about us in proceedings affect our futures profoundly and permanently. We need you to know how to protect and promote our best interests and you will have a better chance of doing this, we think, if you understand more deeply how it feels to be us.

There's plenty of space to take notes, we hope you'll pick up a pen and jot down your thoughts. Dig deep as we've done and start new conversations.

Family Justice Young People's Board
(with Dawn Reeves curator)

Chapter 1

Our experiences of family court proceedings

- A big deal
- All eyes were on me
- It's just a car
- Epic day
- When we're asked
- The day that changed everything

A big deal

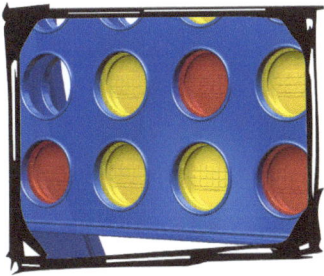

Yesterday I went to sleep confident and self-assured. It was silly that we needed to go to court. What happened wasn't nearly as big a deal as they were making it out to be. I was good with adults and I would be fine. So when I woke up that morning drenched in a cold sweat, I was confused. My heart was racing and I couldn't work out why. I thought 'a cold sweat' was something from stories but I experienced it, and it was disgusting. It couldn't be related to the court appearance. I was strong. It must have been some weird coincidence.

Now my younger brother and I are sitting in a massive conference room, high up, overlooking London. The walls are glass, and we are sitting at a table for 30 people. Mum didn't want us to go to court so here we are, playing Connect 4 with a trainee solicitor who may not have interacted with children since he was a child himself. Lawyers are bustling past. Our parents are in court right now, deciding our future. We never finished our game.

The judge got annoyed. We do have to go to court. Now we are in a small room with a woman we've never met before. She asks us questions about Dad: "Does he hit you?" Pause.

"Are you scared of him?" It's ridiculous. I'm not scared of Dad, that would be stupid. My brother wants to tell a different story, but I shut him down. He doesn't know what he's talking about. Those times didn't hurt. We're fine, it's fine.

"If you don't stop that you can't stay in the room." The woman scares me, she's big and blocking the door. I don't want to leave my brother, he is confused but he is only nine, and I need to protect him. I shut up.

It's the next morning, I'm back in school, I should be back to normal. It's History, and I'm sitting in the middle of a classroom of 12-year-olds who are whispering about Ellie going to court. I shouldn't have mentioned it.

"Why did you go?"

"Did you break the law?"

I explain it was family court.

"What did your parents do? Did they hit you?"

"Are you going into care?"

The teacher starts the lesson, but I am stuck in the middle of the class, already behind, and now I feel like I'm surrounded. Going to court is a much bigger deal than I realised, and that was only one day.

Anonymous

Our message to professionals: Help us understand what happens in proceedings. It's so important we know what's going on. Give us a step-by-step guide.

All eyes were on me

I was 10 years old and my parents had just announced their separation. I was the eldest of two daughters. I'd moved out of the family home with my dad. My sister stayed. Following some disgusting allegations from my mum, I was ordered to attend court.

I was confused and didn't know why I was there. I was walking into the unknown. I don't recall seeing any other children there either. My mum asked Cafcass if she could have some time to speak with me. My dad agreed to this, with my best interests at heart, but warned her of my reaction.

I don't know how else to describe it other than, if you have a phobia of spiders, you wouldn't feel comfortable sitting in a room surrounded by them. Of course, I didn't have a phobia of my mum, but I hadn't seen her since I walked out with my dad.

There was little regard for my feelings, and I kicked off, as my dad had predicted. Cafcass were worried about me being asked to attend the court because they didn't think it was good for me.

I think I was trying to balance the needs and feelings of everyone on my shoulders, putting pressure on myself because I was the eldest child. It was the norm to live with your mum and because I wanted to live with my dad, I felt I was being awkward or difficult. Little did I know that I would be doing that balancing act for years to come.

At that time and in my situation, Cafcass were correct because court was no place for me to be though I don't think that a blanket ban on children in court is the correct philosophy. All children should be encouraged to write a letter to the judge to explain how their family difficulties affect them. The family courts have come a long way since 2010 and the voice of the child is louder than ever before.

If a child attends court to meet the judge, it must be appropriate. And if it's the right time, then it's essential that support is in place: someone to explain why they are there, to keep dialogue open and to reassure us that if they feel uncomfortable at any time that the meeting can be paused. That's what would have helped me.

Anonymous

Our message to professionals: Every child is an individual when it comes to being in court. The situation is dependent on their needs, and they will need time, support and reassurance to meet with a judge. Remember to tell them they can do this.

It's just a car

Stuck. My feet glued to the ground. I am completely motionless as the rubber wheels roll towards me. Panic spreads like a rash, rushing through my toes, coursing up my legs as they begin to tremble.

You can do this. It's just a car.

I try to slow my breathing. Don't cry. It drives past me, the driver not sparing a glance, I go unnoticed. I feel my body relax.

It's just a car.

Repeating this mantra like a chant in my head, I force myself to move from my spot and continue walking. I push the memory far into the back of my mind until my eyelids grow heavy, wearily I start to give into sleep. Next thing I'm back on the pavement, staring wide-eyed at the fast-approaching car. It's just a car. But this time, it doesn't drive past.

A man gets out, the same man I was supposed to idolise and look up to. Smiling down at me, the sweetest smile, as he yanks something from beside me. My sister. She shrieks as she's thrown into the backseat of the car. I try to grab her, but I'm immobilised, unable to scream, run or cry. Standing there powerless, I look around at the faces I am supposed to trust, the faces who were supposed to protect her. And then I wake up.

I felt invisible during the courts, as I do in my nightmares. I felt those who should have had my back somehow weren't able to, leaving me vulnerable with no armour.

It's not like that anymore.

I was given back the control taken away from me. The court proceedings stopped, and no contact was advised, and only on terms set by my sister and me. I am beginning to stand taller when faced with a reminder and my nightmares and panic attacks are decreasing. I suffer from them less and less.

I am stronger, and I am resilient.

Anonymous

Our message for professionals: Don't let us live with conflict any longer than necessary. Listen to us from the start, these experiences have a long-term effect on our lives.

Epic day

Suddenly, one day my case worker asked me if I would like to speak to our district judge. I jumped at the chance and kept my fingers crossed. For as long as I can remember, I had been telling everyone what I wanted, what would make me happy, but nothing seemed to be getting done about it. I was feeling really tired and frustrated. It was a massive weight hanging over me.

My miracle moment came when the judge agreed to meet with me. I thought WOW! This is it, my proper chance to tell my story.

On the day I was so nervous, but I knew the meeting could really help me. So I just told myself that yes, the judge is in charge, but he is also a person, just like me. I spent one hour with him. He let me sit in his posh chair and basically asked what things I liked about my life.

I love tennis, gaming and going to my local theme park, Drayton Manor. I've just read Animal Farm by George Orwell and enjoyed the political content, and my favourite film is the director's cut version of The Justice League.

He asked what things I used to do with my dad, and what my mum would do if I said I wanted to see my dad. It was so good to meet him, he wasn't scary at all and listened to everything I said. It felt amazing. After the meeting I felt proud of myself and relieved that I had spoken to the man that was making the decisions about my life.

Later that day my mum phoned to tell me the judge's decision. I screamed with happiness. I am convinced that because I just told the truth, he believed me and was able to sort everything out. My life was brilliant after that day; I am very happy.

I am 13 now. I do have moments where I dread it happening again, but if it did, I would ask to speak to the judge straight away. No hesitation.

I would like to think that my story could give hope to other children. We all have a voice. We just need the opportunity to have it heard.

Anonymous

Our message to professionals: Help us to meet the decision makers early on.

When we're asked

Some parts of my very first day at school are very easy to remember; others, not so much. I do clearly recall being asked about why I had changed school. Quite a normal question to ask the new kid, I now know. I think, as I was so young, I told my new classmates the facts. I had moved away from my parents who had home-schooled me and moved in with my grandparents who took the decision to enrol me in a school.

Later, two years after my brother and I went into foster care, we were eventually sent to a school nearby. I had become more aware of what people thought of me and had developed some social skills. It was harder for my brother. He was six by then and most of the learning about how to make friends and interact is done at a very early age. Even so, when the question came up again, I said, "Oh, I moved house," and changed the subject.

I didn't really know these people, so why should they know such awkward and personal things? It wasn't a lie exactly, but I wish I'd handled the situation differently. The girl who'd asked is still my best friend five years later. It was a long time before she found out that I was a foster child, even though I'd told my Year Two friends on the first day of school.

It has really only been recently that I have been able to bring the subject of my birth parents up with my best friend, which was difficult, but I felt much better after it had been discussed.

My brother and I agree now. The best way is to just explain things straight away but if you aren't comfortable telling people, or, they ask a lot of questions, it's OK to ask them to stop. It can be overwhelming.

He wants to travel the world and work in the Navy as an engineer. It's good to be able to think of something you really want as it sets you goals for the future, there's something to strive for.

As for me, I'm determined to become a police psychologist. It probably started with the police coming into school, raising awareness of knife crime and being safe online. I could see myself doing a role like that. Now I love understanding what goes on in people's heads, why we do what we do. It combines my interests.

Anonymous

Our message to professionals: Think about what life's like for us at school. Help us think about what information we want to share with our friends and how to share it.

–The day that changed everything–

During one of my last court cases, when my mother took me to court for not wanting contact with her, I met with my guardian and my solicitor. That was the first time I really connected with my case. Before, I'd been held at arm's length and all the important decisions were made for me.

At the Cafcass office, my dad had to stay in the waiting room and I was tossed into the deep end. Led by a member of staff to a huge conference hall, our footsteps echoing, I was overwhelmed. It was so intimidating. There were just three of us in a room with so many empty chairs. I remember fidgeting with my school uniform, feeling so underdressed sitting opposite my guardian and solicitor in their smart suits. There wasn't time to be self-conscious. We got straight down to business, drafting up a permitted contact plan. Some people say that what we discussed wasn't appropriate for a twelve-year-old, but I disagree. I'd been thrown a lifeline. When I said what I wanted, they listened.

With a plan outlined, on my terms, I had more control. It was such a relief. I agreed to emails, and she could attend my skating training and a few small things. It wasn't much, and that was exactly what I needed. I was given the opportunity to talk to the judge before the hearing, and honestly that made a world of difference. I felt the judge really heard, in my own words, how important it was for me.

Throughout the proceedings I met with a lot of professionals. It was always nerve-wracking. I could never be certain of where it would lead, if the outcome would be something I wanted. Being granted the opportunity to draft up my own contact plan – one that I believed my mother would agree to – made all the difference. Our proposal was subsequently agreed in court. That meeting changed my life.

Eventually, my mother became unhappy with the arrangements and a psychological evaluation was ordered for the whole family. The findings led my mother to disengage from court. Now I've had no contact with her for five years. Today I'm much happier, in a house full-time with my dad, step-mum, and step-sister. It's a secure platform from where I can achieve my aspirations. One of my main hopes is to become a political policy advisor and I feel I'm on the right path.

Anonymous

Our message to professionals: **Make sure all plans** *for* **us are made** *with* **us**

You are braver than you think, stronger than you believe

Don't be afraid to ask questions, ask then and there... Don't wait.

Talk to people who care about you... don't bottle it up

There's a big decision being made, you have to know what's going on

can be overwhelming

For professionals

Notice your reaction to the pieces. Which experiences stand out or resonate with you? And why?

Think back to your first time in family court proceedings? How did you feel? How do you spot what the children and young people are feeling? How could you open up space to communicate better in formal settings?

In these stories, young people are sharing very personal information, thoughts and feelings about what they need and hope for. When you have disclosed something of yourself, what impact did it have?

Think about a time when you've had to advocate for your own needs or when you've challenged others, stood up for what you believe in? What was difficult? What helped?

What inspires you about the pieces and what might you do differently as a result of having read them?

What could you do differently to make family proceedings more positive and understandable for the children and young people with whom you work?

Key takeaways...

- Help us understand what happens in family court proceedings, step by step. Check in all the time to make sure that we know what is happening and why.

- Help us to understand the reasons behind the recommendations that you make and record our thoughts about them in your reports.

- Help us to meet the decision makers early on.

- Make sure all plans for us are made *with* us.

Chapter 2

Our experiences of family conflict

- My life is fixable
- 16/11
- Growing
- Cheese Sauce, No Remorse
- After the fear
- Chess piece
- When will this be over?

My life is fixable

For the first four years of my life, I lived with my parents in Yemen. I was brought up as Muslim and I moved around a lot. My grandad had migrated to the UK in the 1950s, my grandma joined him, and they later adopted me.

In 2010, the court proceedings for the adoption ended and cracks appeared. Home life was miserable, and I knew no English. At school I struggled through Year Seven but was fluent in English by Year Eight.

My grandad was abusive, controlled all the money and said I must call him Dad. He silenced me and told me not to tell the school about my parents or my life in Yemen. I spoke out for years, but I wasn't properly protected by those professionals around me.

When I returned from the mosque, he would be sitting down with the Quran on his lap. He forced me to kneel and if I didn't, he would hit me and force me to the floor. He would always make me repeat things from the Quran.

Once, when my grandad was angry, he went into the kitchen where my grandma was cooking, picked up a large knife and said, "I am going to kill you and chop your neck off."

He tried to drag me into the kitchen, but I fought against him and held onto the doorframe with everything I had. My grandma got in his way and stopped him. I was scared for my life. I thought I was going to be murdered.

Grandma was my saviour, she protected me. At that point I contacted police, professionals, and teachers. Social workers and police officers came to the home. I eventually went to live with my foster carers in a safe home.

I am grateful to be safe and happy. I am proud of my achievements. While in foster care, I passed my GCSEs and went to college. In my first year, I achieved numerous awards for the best student union officer of the year, star of the college and more. I play professional cricket for Lancashire and I've trained with the England squad. If I can do this, others can too.

Anonymous

Our message to professionals: Notice the signs of abuse and take the necessary actions to protect us.

16/11

We were two young children thrown into a pitch-black room trying to peep through the curtains to the outside world. It was so close, but we were trapped. Other youngsters were soaking up the sun, spending Father's Day with their dads, going home to somewhere that was familiar and warm. All we could do was sit and watch from a house that felt like it was shivering, an unsafe, terrifying, dark house that could never be a home.

A few weeks later we saw a glimmer of light. The soft glow of our dad's headlights, beaming through the gloomy winter night. Like a flickering projector showing a homecoming movie, we had a feeling of escape.

Except that moment was followed by fiery, flashing police car lights. They'd pass right, like they always do. Because going home isn't a crime?

The startling police lights stopped outside. The comforting glow of dad's car went dead, disappeared in an instant. A dark cloud suddenly formed. The adults were all outside shouting. Dad was taken into the police car. Our mother had called the police.

Our most vivid memory is flicking the lamp on and off, to signal that we needed help. But no-one came. The people who had the power to intervene just didn't see us. Mum turned the police against Dad. He was driven away and told not to come back. Our source of hope and light was snatched away.

That day felt so surreal, hazy, and intense all at once. At nine years old, it was so shocking to see our mum behaving like that. We struggled to understand because up to then, we loved and trusted her. Why weren't we listened to? Our world was turned upside down.

16/11 was the start of a dark, long, and unexpected journey. We had to really persevere to be heard, eventually finding our own solicitor. Why? Why did it take so long?

In the end, the court gave full custody to our father. It has taken a long time for us to learn to express emotions. We've learnt that when we're discussing something, sometimes emotions will be coming from somewhere else. As sisters we are good at different things, but together we're determined, hardworking, meticulous, and sensitive.

Anonymous

Our message to professionals: Listen and genuinely hear us, because it has real life impact. Trust that we know what we want, even if we're young. Represent what we are saying no matter what your interpretation. Also, think about what a child is not saying to you, do they feel afraid to talk to you?

Growing

I'm five. Daddy shouts at us a lot – Mummy, me, and my brother. He gets so angry he slams the car all over the road and makes Mummy get out of the car. He tells her to walk home but we're ages from home. We scream and cry and try to get out to walk with her. Eventually, he lets Mummy back in. It feels wrong being happy in a situation like this, but Mummy's back and we feel safe.

I'm seven. Mummy and Daddy tell us they're doing something called a 'divorce.' It means we won't all live together anymore. I ask if that means I get two birthdays and Christmases (it does!). Somehow, 'splitting up' doesn't sound like a bad thing. So long as I live with Mummy, I don't really mind it.

I'm nine and I'm used to the court order now. I go to my dad's Wednesday night and Friday night. Daddy always tells us how much he fought for us or how much money he paid someone called a barrister. He doesn't get up in the morning to make us breakfast. The courts didn't really seem to care about that.

I'm 11 and I'm just starting high school. Like that isn't hard enough, I have Dad to deal with too. Sometimes he gets so angry that he throws things. I have to explain to every new friend that I have two phones. I don't tell them it's because I think my dad bugged all our phones. They just think I'm spoiled and like having two phones.

I'm 15 and he chases me through the house. He's like an animal. He screams and shouts. I barricade myself in my room but he's stronger, he bursts through, twisting the door, breaking the chest of drawers, and shattering my mirror. I want to call the police, to get out, to go home… but I'm glued to my bed. I can't move.

I'm 22 and he doesn't control me anymore. I can say 'no' now because he can't do anything anymore. Saying no is still hard. I worry about having to say no in the future: to birthdays, to my graduation. I tell myself I don't want to get married because it's easier than having that argument. Every time I say no, I remind myself that I am strong, I have control, and I have a choice.

Anonymous

Our message to professionals: Make sure all circumstances are correctly taken into consideration when deciding the outcome of custody battles. Professionals need to take the time to correctly assess the situation before placing children into conflict environments.

Cheese Sauce, No Remorse

Teatime, The Simpsons buzzes in the background.
Mums not here, dad's cooking. What's that smell? I hate it.
.Cheese? maybe parmesan?
He brings the plate closer; the sick smell clots the air.
I'm in tears, I hate cheesy pasta.
But he already knew that.

"Eat it now! I'll sit here until you're done. Make sure it's all gone."
The Simpsons is off now. All focus is on me.
Choking it down, crying into my food, "Daddy, please, come on."
I say to myself, "deep breaths, don't vomit."
Even the bacon pieces can't save me, I can't stomach cheese sauce,
"You'll eat it, don't waste it, I don't care if you don't want it."

It seems silly.
But I was 5 then, and I'm 22 now.
I still can't stomach cheese sauce,
He has no remorse.

Anonymous

After the fear

Whenever I had to see my dad, I'd struggle to sleep for days before. On the day that I had to see him, I'd wake up feeling shaky and nauseous and just wished that it would all stop. I never wanted to see my dad. I knew what he was like when he stopped acting because people were around.

He liked to be commanding, controlling, and dominant. Although Mum and I got away, he used his right to see me to make sure we weren't truly free. For years as a child I felt scared. I had no control over my life and decisions about me were made by strangers. I remember one time I had to see him and the family court adviser (FCA) came with us. I was scared but knew that at least he wouldn't do anything because she was there and we were out in public. I really didn't want to be there, but I was always told that I had to go and didn't have a choice.

We were at a big park and garden and, as always, he grabbed onto my hand so tight it hurt. While we walked around, he chatted with the FCA. I felt really alone. At one point she started asking me questions as he walked behind us and I knew he could hear what we were talking about. She asked, "How often would you like to see your dad?"

I replied, "Never."

I felt so scared saying that but knew that I had to say how I felt.

"But we've had such a nice day."

I looked at the floor, my chest tight.

"And he's made such an effort to see you." She made me feel guilty.

So eventually I gave in and said if I really had to, "I'd see him for 30 minutes."

I felt an icy cold shock when the court was told that I'd said, "I liked to see my father."

Such a subtle twisting of words made a huge difference.

The times I had to see my dad are some of the clearest memories I have of my childhood. Most people look back to when they were a child with fond memories, lots of mine though are frightening.

I remember the day my mum said I would never have to see him again. I was so happy. But it took years before that happened. And those years left their mark.

Anonymous

Our message to professionals: Make sure we can talk without being overheard. Check I'm not feeling pressured. Don't pressurise me. Hear what I have to say.

Chess piece

"He loves you. Your father does love you, you know."

I was told this a lot growing up. This same statement circled round and round in my mind. Love? A concept that seemed so far away from what I was experiencing. This, this is love? For a child, it was hard to understand when your world was being flipped upside down. Why was a man who supposedly loved me, doing the things he was doing? Why did a man who loved me vow to destroy my family's life?

I wanted to scream. Scream at the professionals for making assumptions. How could they possibly know? Scream at myself, maybe I was to blame? Perhaps they were right, and I just didn't understand? I felt guilty, as if it was my fault these things were happening. I wanted to scream at him too. If he loved me like everyone seemed to claim, why couldn't he show it?

Confused and frustrated, I just wanted to scream.

I was a pawn, a piece used in a game of strategy. Dehumanised. I didn't matter outside of the game. I was no longer seen as a child with their own mind, thoughts, and feelings. I was an object. An object my father owned and had a right to see, entirely in his possession.

My father didn't love me. At least not in the way people repeatedly informed me. It was possession. Maybe in some way he thought it was love and truly believed it. However, it is not as black and white as that. And possession is not love.

Anonymous

Our message to professionals: Professionals shouldn't make assumptions; they should ask questions. Look for evidence and get a true understanding of the wishes and feelings of each child you work with.

When will this be over?

I hate tuna pasta, can't stand the smell or the taste of the stuff. During the time I was forced to live with my birth mother, it was her go-to meal, and even now it makes me sick. It's funny how that stays with you.

My twin sister and I were only 11 when she stopped us properly seeing our dad for five months. I was so young and didn't know what was going on between my parents. I just knew that they were arguing over me and my twin, and it wasn't good.

It was during the first court case, when my parents agreed to work with Cafcass. My birth mum got it written into the proceedings that my twin and I could only see our dad for two nights every other week. Neither me nor my twin were told what was going on. We were only told when we would spend time with dad. It was super scary. The nights that we spent with our dad and step-mum were the only joy in my life at the time.

My life at my birth mother's house was a living hell. We were always low on toiletries like soap, shampoo, and deodorant and she wouldn't have enough food to feed us properly, even though she had enough money. Our packed lunches were made from the last night's leftovers and if we didn't eat the packed lunch, we would have it again the next day.

During those five months she and I would argue relentlessly. Sometimes it would be about my dad and the court proceedings; sometimes it would be about other things like her not letting me quit the clarinet.

Once we argued from the crack of dawn until it was time for bed. My birth mum did not like me telling my step-mum that I loved and missed her. She was furious and kicked off. She took away the phone my dad bought for me to use to contact him, and she went through all the messages between us. I wasn't allowed any electronics or to even talk to my twin sister. The only thing I could do was sit in my room alone. I cried and panicked myself sick.

Anonymous

Our message to professionals: Nothing about me without me! I need to be the first to know what's happening. And signpost children and young people to other support services who we can reach out to when needed.

Even if you think it won't – it will get better

You are not at fault in all this, you are loved

You don't always have to be strong for everyone else

Relationships are messy, living with conflict is hard, look after yourself

It's ok to say you're struggling, to feel hurt or angry, whatever you think or feel is ok, Your feelings can change, that's ok

For professionals

Which pieces in this chapter do you connect with? Which resonate with your experience of young people dealing with family conflict? Any details that stand out?

In both your own family life and professional life, how do you respond to conflict? Has your approach to conflict changed over time?

What influences the choices you make when those around you are disagreeing?

Take a moment to reflect on your own listening practice. What gets in the way of really good listening? Do you check out what you think you have heard from the young people with whom you are working? If you don't, why not?

How can you help show that different ways of communication and behaviour are possible? That different futures are possible – even in the most challenging of situations?

What are the strengths that help you work in situations where there is significant conflict? Where might you need to change the way you or your organisation work?

Key takeaways…

- Listen and genuinely hear us because this is what will make the most difference.

- Represent what we are saying no matter what your interpretation. Don't make assumptions, look for evidence.

- Why is it ok for me to live with the conflict in my family any longer than is necessary?

Chapter 3

Our diverse experiences

- Alphabet soup
- High spirits
- All about me
- My story is mine
- A third-party result
- A family who love me
- 1000 things at once

Alphabet soup

When I first met my Cafcass representative, they used my birth name, not the name I am called. I didn't know them well enough to feel comfortable correcting them. I was scared they would judge me and it might make things difficult. I didn't like meeting my guardian, and when I was discussed by the adults, they used the wrong pronouns and it felt like they couldn't see me. They were dealing with, trying to help, a person that didn't actually exist. I was forced to become their image of me, and nothing felt real.

Last year, I met a new guardian for the first time.

She introduced herself and asked how I liked to be referred to. I gave my name, the one I chose, the one my mum and friends use. She smiled. I think someone must have spoken to her about my pronouns, because she asked for them too, and I said they/them. She nodded and didn't ask me any more questions. I left the meeting feeling listened to and respected, and I didn't dread the next one. When she talks to me, I can relax and open up. Occasionally she has got my pronouns wrong, but she always corrects herself and apologises straight away. It hasn't happened in a long time now.

When I meet new people, she's with me and introduces me with my name and pronouns. It always makes me smile. I think it surprises some adults, but nobody says anything. I know that if they did, she would defend me. Nobody is telling me I'm not old enough to know about myself, so I can relax and open up. I need to share how I feel because it's important to my case. But when I'm called by the wrong name, I close up like a clam in a shell and it's harder for me to trust the people I need to.

Recently, she asked if I could give her some advice about how to talk to non-binary children. I agreed and we drafted a kind of script for other Cafcass professionals to use. I'm excited to think it could help other people like me feel safer during the court process, which is very stressful anyway.

Anonymous

Our message to professionals: Respect, consideration and support from guardians is essential. Ask us what we want to be called. Think about the resources you use and make sure they are not gendered.

Check if our parents, or foster carers, family or friends know we identify as nonbinary. If support is needed, then find local specialists.

High Spirits

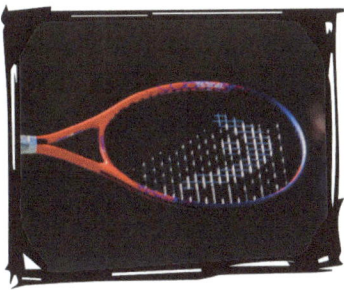

I was nine years old when I heard about the Family Justice Young People's Board (FJYPB). I thought it would be an amazing experience. I always wanted the chance to work in a group alongside other young people. Current members of the group helped put me at ease during my interview. I was asked to give a presentation and I chose to do this on children with disabilities playing sports. I was asked lots of questions.

Waiting to hear back was incredibly nerve-wracking. When I finally got the acceptance letter through the post I was ecstatic and my heart was pounding. I was invited to London for my induction before becoming an official member of the FJYPB.

Since then, I have participated in many projects. For the 'In My Shoes' work, I took the opportunity to write a poem, 'After all, it's all about me'. I received a lot of support from other team members. They played a crucial role in helping boost my confidence before the big day when I read my poem on stage. I was very nervous and anxious at the thought of speaking in front of lots of other people, but I read my poem clearly and everyone seemed to enjoy it.

It wasn't as daunting as I thought. I was very proud of myself and happy that I'd done it. The experience meant I became noticed for the work I was doing. I was asked to write top tips for working with children with disabilities, and to be a part of a team creating a toolkit to help staff. It has been one of my biggest achievements to date.

It's important that anyone working in family justice includes people with disabilities in the decision-making processes. I enjoy being an advocate for others going through the same thing.

I'm 15 now. When I'm older I want to be a neurosurgeon and a Paralympian wheelchair tennis player.

Anonymous

Our message to professionals: Give us the right support and help us to support others and we will surprise you and help you do better for children and young people!

After all, it's all about me

It's my life
It's my family
It's my future
I speak with my feelings
I write with my mind
Listen to my words
Communicate with me
Include me in decisions involving my life
After all it's about me

Include us all
Big or small
Brown or white
No matter what we look like.
Listen and value us
Don't dismiss us

I need to speak
I need you to understand how I feel
Value and respect my feelings
I want you to listen

Before you make your decision
And take a position
After all it's all about me

I feel sick
I feel weak
To me my future is bleak,
It's time for you to speak.
I place my trust in you
Help me
Listen to me
Speak for me when I cannot

Tell me decisions that have been made
Update me at every stage
Don't run away
Don't ignore me
Speak plain
Take time to explain and engage

After all it's all about me
This is my life
Don't forget this about me
Don't forget me

Anonymous

My story is mine

I slam my door, pressing my back against the old wood and try to breathe again. Mum doesn't believe me. I can hear her stomping away in anger. I begin to doubt myself, but no! I can't think like that. I know what I said, and I know what the social worker told me. It's not my fault if he told mum something different. I just wish she'd believe me.

It's not the first time this has happened. The social worker says it's because he knows better, he's seen this type of case before. But he can't have. That's not possible, because it's mine.

Mum and I fight a lot, we get into arguments about who said what. The social worker seems to tell two different stories, one to me and one to her. Like I wouldn't notice. Sometimes he says things and I think, I never said that or that's not what I wanted. We mainly meet online via laptop, and sometimes I have to fight the urge to shout at him through the screen and say really bad words.

We are in our home country, visiting family for Easter. Mum gasps, and I look up, she's gone all pale and her hand trembles around her phone.

"The social worker," she says. My tummy drops. It's never good news.

My sister looks first at mum and then me, and then gets up and quietly leaves. She hates being involved; it makes her cry. Mum reads the email to me, her voice wavering, and I blink at her in a daze. It doesn't make sense. She's not abducted me. I wanted to come too. We were never told we couldn't leave. And now my social worker says if we return to England, mum could be arrested.

We decided to stay. I don't think there is a case anymore. No more social workers. For a long time, there wasn't a day that went by without me having to think about my social worker, and what was happening to my family. It was a scary time, and I was always worried about what would happen to us.

It's hard to imagine, when you're in the middle of it, that things can change. Life can and does get better. I know the social worker meant to help us. He was there to move our lives along so my sister and I could have a more normal and settled childhood. But it felt like he was holding us all back. I'm thankful that days can pass now when I don't think about it at all.

Anonymous

Our message to professionals: Please share information accurately and tell us what will be shared with others, including parents.

Remember to keep children and young people informed about what is happening to them. Help us feel safe, not scared.

A third-party result

Our plane didn't just depart for England. For me and family it marked a departure from my controlling father. England was supposed to be a fresh start. That's what I'd hoped for, but it turned into a new nightmare. I hadn't escaped anything; I'd just moved locations. My father spread lies to the authorities that my siblings and I had been brainwashed and kidnapped, when in reality this never happened. He was everything to everyone, but not a father to us.

This nightmare made me feel like I was going insane. It felt like I was being treated like a criminal. The police took my passport, preventing me from visiting my mother country and at times I struggled to prove who I was. School trips and days abroad were ruined because of the situation my father created and that everyone seemed to believe.

I became a third party in a Hague Convention case. This was a very unique and scary experience, but the only solution to my case. I remember sitting in the High Court in my school uniform. I was annoyed because it meant I was missing more days off school. The judge's decision would affect the rest of my life, and if that wasn't stressful enough, my English wasn't the best and I couldn't understand the difficult legal terms.

I had to learn to interpret the case through my solicitors and my mother's facial expressions. The faded whispers of my father's translator echoed through the courtroom, giving me clues about the state of my future. Although it was daunting, after feeling voiceless for months, I was glad to have this opportunity to be heard.

After many years, my feelings and wishes were eventually acknowledged by both the judge and my father. The case had a damaging effect on my mental health and ruined my relationship with my father and his family. Maybe if I was listened to from the start the proceedings would have been shorter, easier, and less stressful. Perhaps my family wouldn't have become divided, viewing each other as enemies.

Not every child gets the opportunity to become a third party in their own case, and if they can't, what else can we do to give them the voice and representation that they all deserve?

Anonymous

Our message for professionals: Don't leave me to guess what's going on. My voice needs to be heard and I need to be able to express it in my first language.

I need to understand what is being said and happening about me and my life. Think about using an interpreter for a child in court.

A family who love me

At school I was called names. People said I was weird, crazy and a psycho. They made racist comments about my dark skin. They said that life would be better without me in it. I moved schools but by then my mental ill-health was already severe. I didn't feel like I was part of this world.

During my time in a mental health hospital, my parents were in court, trying to adopt me. The local authority didn't want that. I still don't know why. I have the right to a family. They played mind games with me. I was told my adoptive parents didn't want me and that they'd given up on me. I was discouraged from the adoption. Social services and my birth father didn't think I should be adopted by two women. They believed a gay couple couldn't provide everything needed to raise a child. In court, they interrogated my parents for five hours.

I was in hospital during the proceedings and my Cafcass guardian was honest and open with me. She kept me up to date, ensuring I didn't feel alone. She knew the local authorities weren't being completely fair, and she made sure the judge kept her updated in case she needed to intervene on my behalf. When I was released, she made sure I was provided with proper holdalls for my possessions, rather than the binbags I'd been given. She fought for me and made sure I wasn't overlooked because I was in care.

Without the support of my Cafcass guardian, my solicitor, and my mums, I wouldn't have got through it. My dogs, Poppy and Tila, helped too! Throughout my journey, I've endured a lot of mistreatment and injustice. I suffered from the lack of control and power. I was misunderstood by the professionals responsible for my life. The local authority never met my needs, and critical support for my mental ill health was badly delayed. I felt like social services used my vulnerability to their advantage and I was neglected. Social services are still in my life, an aspect I'd hoped would end.

Being adopted was the greatest gift anyone has ever given me. I feel secure knowing that no matter what the future brings, I have my family who loves and supports me.

Anonymous

Our message to professionals: **Don't let your personal prejudices get in the way of my best interests**

1000 things at once

I've had my watch for five years now and even though it's scratched and worn I still love it. I never take it off. It was expensive and I was proud to pay for it myself; I worked really hard to get it. From the age of 13 I was buying and selling Blackberrys and phones on the internet. I had to.

When I was 18, I was kicked out of home. People said I wasn't really kicked out because my dad paid the rent on a flat for me. My mates thought it was cool, but it was just a shell, the only thing in it was a mattress. They'd come round and hang out, but when the door closed I was alone.

It was only because I had the courage and motivation to start my own events business that I had enough money to live on. If I'd had a normal nine-to-five job I probably wouldn't have been able to survive. I had to pay for all the bills and to furnish my flat. I really had no idea what I was doing at the start.

On the surface it could look like I've had this fantastic life. I've travelled the world and had amazing experiences. But all of that is a distraction as far as I'm concerned. It's irrelevant. I've never had the love and support of caring parents, someone to look after me, to pat me on the back and say you can do it.

I've been beaten up – physically and emotionally abused since I was 12. Sometimes it feels like my head is in a blender; I'm not sure who I am or what to do. My dad belittles me, says my business has no potential, calls me a leech, and thinks that I should be able to buy my own place. Financial control is a way he controls me and my brothers.

This is something the social workers, judges and other professionals in the family justice system don't seem to get. I moved back home because he provided all the basics: food, schoolbooks and a phone. It gave him the perfect chance to say to the social worker, "Well, all my children live with me so it can't be that bad." My dad is abusive and manipulative. They see the so-called glamourous lifestyle and make the wrong assumptions. Everyone is different.

Having the chance to be on the FJYPB has built my confidence and opened my eyes. Success is about being happy and feeling free to follow your own path. Although Covid hit my business badly, I'm determined to make it work. No matter how many times I look at my watch, there's never enough time.

Anonymous

Our message to professionals: Don't make assumptions about the lifestyle of children and families. Get to know our individual needs.

Just be you

...y how it feels to be in your shoes

...n't feel ashamed, we're all different, with different needs,
ask for what you need

Don't give up, it's weird but going through negative stuff does make you stronger

Be hopeful, even if you feel you can't, try to be hopeful

...ou can exceed expectations

For professionals

What impact has reading these pieces had on you? What surprises you about the experiences of the young people?

What about you might other people see as different, even if that's your norm? How has this affected you?

Think of a moment in your career when your views have been challenged, or you've challenged the preconceived views of others. What happened? What helped or didn't in that situation?

Reflect on how different types of privilege or discrimination play out in the family justice system?

What ideas do you have about how could we change things so that children and young people don't experience discrimination and different treatment in the family justice system?

What else could you do in your practice to help make this positive change?

Key takeaways…

- Take the time to find out about our needs. Don't make assumptions. Instead, tailor resources and information to our needs.

- Don't let your personal prejudices get in the way of my best interests.

- Give us the right support, we will surprise you.

Chapter 4

Our experiences of health and well-being

- Helping others
- A web of support
- Mental health marathon
- Dear Diary
- In a goldfish bowl
- Starting again
- The hard way

Helping others

I was six months old when my parents split up. I haven't had contact with my dad since then. Although, when I was eight, my dad got in touch with the courts to request contact. I found out that he decided not to go ahead with it once he knew I was being assessed for my Asperger's.

When I was younger, I felt sad about not being able to see my dad. The last time he tried to contact me I gave him all my contact information, but even then, he didn't even contact me once. After that I no longer counted him as my father.

Since I was 12, I've been a carer for my mum who has fibromyalgia and other illnesses. Being a young carer is both hard and easy.

One of the hardest parts is seeing my mum in pain and not being able to do the things she once was able to do. I have to make sure Mum takes her meds and that she doesn't pick up something that's too heavy for her. And I remind her to not do too much, or she'll be in pain the next day.

One of the easy bits is driving my mum around and the days when Mum is unwell, we'll watch a movie or a show together.

I like to help with doing the dishes after dinner or getting the washing out of the machine or putting it in. I walk the dogs and I've set up her accounts, such as online banking payments. It's become normal now because I have been doing this for 10 years.

The things I really enjoy are looking after my pets, helping people, playing games and the voluntary/paid work I do. I worry about the future and moving out. That would mean Mum is at home alone, so some of the chores that I do now will slowly start going back to her. Being Mum's carer has influenced my decision about which university to attend because I do not want to be too far away. I also wonder how, with my Asperger's, I'll find it being in bigger class sizes.

My ambitions are to work in the cyber security industry. I'm about to start studying my course at university this September. I know it will be hard, but I'm looking forward to it.

Anonymous

Our message to professionals: Understand my needs and what roles and responsibilities I have at home. Sometimes I won't ask for help.

A web of support

Alex: seen Bradley today?? he didn't turn up to form
Lucie: not in maths either, maybe he'll come in at lunch? he's been having more of those meetings

Alex sends a fingers crossed emoji, then pockets his phone and heads to his next class. Bradley doesn't share much, and Alex isn't about to push, but he knows his friend's parents are divorcing and it's getting messy. Sometimes Bradley is pulled out of class and he is rarely around anymore to go biking in the park after school. Teachers excuse his missed homework. For any other reason, Alex would be insanely jealous, but it kinda just makes him a bit sad.

Still, he tries to keep Bradley updated on what he misses. Not the schoolwork, the fun stuff, the dramas in class, who said what, funny stories. Bradley doesn't always answer his messages, but Alex thinks it's appreciated. Lucie's the same. They try to keep him in the loop, make stuff feel a bit more normal.

Lucie says Bradley shouted at her a few weeks ago. He's never done that before. It was over something stupid too –

forgetting to save an extra seat during dinner. She'd been upset, but they had both agreed it wasn't really Bradley's fault. More like he's going through something real tough, and he probably couldn't help lashing out a bit.

Alex wishes there's something he could do to help. The school has been good. It's not just the teachers cutting Bradley some slack. He's got a support officer that he disappears with sometimes, and he always comes back looking happier. More like himself. There's a friendly looking woman too. Bradley says she's from Cafcass, not part of the school.

Bradley: where are you

                                        Alex: by music, you coming in?

Bradley: Yeah, mum just dropped me off

                                                            Alex: Cool

                                      Alex: Everything alright?

Bradley: dunno yet, ill tell you in a bit

Alex waves when Bradley comes around the corner, head down, plodding along. He's found a bench, wondering if Bradley has something important to say. He's never really acknowledged everything that's happening. Maybe Bradley feels ready to share? He wishes Lucie was here; she's better at stuff like this. But he's gonna try his best and listen.

Anonymous

Our message to professionals: Ask me if I want school to know what is happening in my life so they can support me. Consideration and coordination with the school can help everything run more smoothly.

Mental health marathon

In 2013, after I disclosed some serious issues about my past, my mental health started declining. It wasn't just an instant feeling that happened overnight. It started with small things.

I stopped watching movies that I had always loved. My favourite food didn't taste like it used to. Athletics has always been a big part of my life. I used to train hard. In 2012 I was named as one of the fastest sprinters in the UK. I lost interest in everything. My life moved out of the fast lane and into slow motion.

I got into trouble at school. I was paranoid, seeing things, obsessive, and suffering extreme anxiety. Everything seemed like too much. I felt alienated. To cope, I started self-harming. I felt so empty. I blamed myself for feeling like this. Once I started putting myself and others around me in dangerous situations, my parents had no option but to call the police and I got taken to CAMHS. Initially I wasn't assessed under the Mental Health Act. Instead, social services placed me in a children's home. In the home I felt even more paranoid and I started having panic attacks.

I found out later that I wasn't placed in the right care. I got assessed in 2016 and detained in a mental health hospital. In hospital I was put in isolation, which felt like prison. I struggled as there was nobody to help me feel 'normal'. Although this was a very difficult time in my life, it was the only place where I could start to get better. If I had been placed there sooner, maybe my mental health wouldn't have deteriorated as much as it did. I have positive memories of my time in hospital as well. It was there with the support of my Cafcass guardian and the courts that I was able to get confirmation I had been adopted.

My mental health has taken over my life and it's not something I can run away from. I still have a long way to go, but I am already so far from where I used to be and I'm proud of that. Just because you're struggling doesn't mean you're failing!

Anonymous

Our message to professionals: I'm not a statistic, I'm a person. Take time to get to know me, and if you don't have time, fight for it!

Dear Diary…

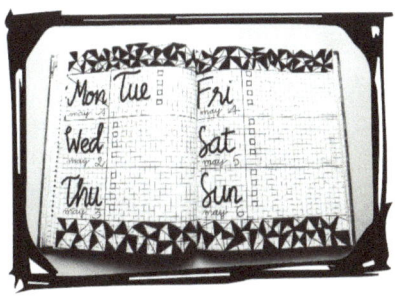

I've just finished my first week in lockdown. It's actually not that bad. A week off work, off school. I could so get used to this. It's strange not seeing Mum. She's a high-risk patient so we're not allowed to see her for a while. I know we live with our dad anyway, but it feels weird.

Dear Diary…
We've been in lockdown for a few months now. It's tough but there's talk of ending some restrictions just before summer, so that's good. If it happens.

I'm starting uni soon, exciting! I've been able to do some work online so I've some money saved up for summer.

Trying to stay positive. The NHS is amazing. But it's hard. I worry what the lifting of restrictions will mean for my mum? She's still high-risk. I'm anxious too. I've gained a bit of weight. There's been nothing else to do other than eat on the sofa. Ugh… just in time for summer too. I don't know how I feel about going out and seeing everyone else.

Dear Diary…
I spend my days scrolling through social media. I can see everything I'm not. I probably enjoyed Eat Out to Help Out a bit too much. I love sports, but I can't train. I can't see my friends, or socialise. We just entered another lockdown and I can't even go stand at my mum's window anymore.

I've started uni but it's online, so I don't know anyone. I spend most of days in my room. I honestly don't see the point of it anymore. I feel really alone.

Dear Diary…
It's lockdown day one hundred and … I honestly don't even know anymore. I've lost count or lost interest in counting? I've been waking up at 1pm. I feel guilty for sleeping in and wasting the day, but it's not like I do anything anyway. I'm exhausted.

I've stopped going to half of my zoom lectures now. What's the point? On the one hand, I'm missing human contact, but on the other, I couldn't think of anything worse than having to go out and interact with real people again.

Christmas will be our first one without Mum.

Dear Diary…
We made it as nice as it could be. And it was OK. After this year, I can cope with anything. Thanks for being there. But please, send us a happier new year.

Anonymous

Our message for professionals: On top of the stress of proceedings, the pandemic has had an impact on us. Covid has doubled the pressure.

In a goldfish bowl

One day, my Head of Year took me out of my maths class and into her office. It was small, hot, smelt like coffee and had glass walls. She sat me down and made general conversation about my day until she got a phone call. Someone was here to see me. She left the room. I stared out at the corridor as a woman with short blonde hair and a pair of round black glasses arrived. It was the psychologist.

During my second court case, my birth mum demanded that me, my twin sister and my dad have an assessment. I was 12 and I had no choice but to stay. The psychologist introduced herself and explained what she was there for. I only hummed in reply. She began by asking me about my parents, and where I wanted to live. Before long, I was overwhelmed and could hardly answer. Then I started to cry. It was harder and harder to breathe, but she didn't stop, just kept firing more questions at me. Eventually she offered me a tissue, but I refused and took one from my school bag.

The bell went and my year group were trooping past and staring in at us. I was red with embarrassment and knew everyone was going to ask me why I was there. I felt trapped.

Next, I had to draw two islands, one near and one far away. On the first island I had to put the people I wanted to see and on the distant island the people I didn't. I drew my birth mum on the far away island. The psychologist asked why, and I said, "I don't like her, she hurts the ones I love."

There were a few more questions and then she closed her horrible notepad. I was thanked and told to get my sister. I was free from that room but scared for my sister as she had to do the same thing without me and I couldn't protect her.

Sometimes I go back and read the report from that morning, that time; it brings up many negative memories. In the end though, it's a reminder that things do get better and I'm in a better place.

Anonymous

Our message to professionals: Think about how it felt to be in that situation (overwhelmed, in an emotional state, with no privacy and asked to be responsible for bringing a sister to meet the psychologist). Think about where and when you meet with children and be responsive to their needs. School sometimes isn't the best place for assessments.

Starting again

I was forced to grow up way ahead of time so that I could be a mother and father to my siblings. My beautiful brothers and sisters were, and still are, my pride and joy. Some are still with me, some miles apart and some buried under the soil we now walk upon. I was their backbone, like the pages in an old book held together by the sturdy spine, keeping everything together when I was crumbling apart.

I've always had to learn fast and adapt to different situations quickly. Knowing when to speak and what to say to avoid confrontation or disappointment. I tried my best to mould myself to societal expectations, to be the daughter that my father wanted. But no matter how many hours I spent taking care of everyone, it was never enough. Every day was just another day, somehow scraping by and just existing. I wished for it all to end.

This was all down to 'family honour'. You'd think that we were living in medieval times but things like this actually exist. I wasn't what was accepted. Therefore, I had ruined the family honour. I didn't realise that I'd spend so many years feeling broken, seeking constant validation, approval and endless reassurance from everyone and everything.

Every social worker, every teacher that pried open the hurt, the fear, the constant pain and questions about bruises, assured me that I wouldn't get into trouble. They promised. But somehow it seemed my confidentiality didn't matter to them. I felt I didn't matter.

Each day I would try and be better and kid myself that it would get easier. But in reality, I just got better at managing the ache, the failure. You learn how to smile wider and convince people that you are OK.

Lockdown was the first time in my life when everything stopped. I was tired of being broken and living with it. I wanted to be more. I wanted to see if I could be enough for me.

So, I started over. I stopped living with my dad. I had grieved and mourned my brother for five years. It was easier and somewhat lighter to breathe.

Today I have a life worth living. I am happy to live my life and I got married. I decided the kind of life I want for myself and for my future children.

Anonymous

Our message to professionals: Don't make us feel like we're just another case on an already busy workload. Situations at home have already had a major impact on our emotions and feelings. Help make things better not worse.

Don't promise confidentiality if you can't deliver it, your decisions and words have repercussions.

The hard way

I'll never forget that day. It started off as normal. I was going to get a filling at the dentist. I remember feeling tiny in the big dentist chair and loved the way it reclined.

The next thing I remember was the pain. It was agony. I'd had an injection, my mouth was numb, but I could feel the drilling of my teeth. The pain was unbearable. To this day I still hate that clinical dentist smell. That day, aged nine, I found out that I was immune to anaesthetics.

It was from that diagnosis that I was able to find out about my other medical conditions. My conditions became more prominent as the years progressed. I suffer from postural orthostatic tachycardia, which causes me to experience dizziness, fainting and frequent changes in blood pressure. I also suffer from Ehlers-Danlos, which means I experience chronic pain and tiredness. And I also suffer from insomnia.

One of the main struggles that came with my diagnoses was acceptance; both from myself and the professionals in my life. In the beginning, social workers didn't believe me. I was accused of making up what I was going through. It was one of the hardest times of my life, and it took its toll on me emotionally.

Along with managing the correct pain medication, I've learnt to overcome my personal struggles. My voice matters. I know that I can't always do things in the way that others might, but being acknowledged and getting the correct help allowed me to get to a better place.

Now I'm able to view things from different points of view and I respect others' perspectives. I want to work with young people to help them through situations like this.

Looking back, I wish I could tell my younger self that everything would be OK. I would tell her to have a stronger voice and be more confident. In time she will get the help she needs.

Anonymous

Our message for professionals: Always listen to the children you are working with. Help us to feel confident enough to express our wishes and feelings.

I know you feel like you're alone, but, trust me you aren't

yourself first, (we know it won't be easy)

feelings changed a lot, I learnt it was ok

We can come across a certain way when that's not how we're feeling,

professionals can't always see how we're feeling

Communicate however you can, to get the support you need

For professionals

Which of these experiences of mental and physical health stand out to you? And why?

How do you use empathy to take action to meet the needs of young people?

Think of a hard time in your life when your health and well-being suffered, how did you cope with this? Was it hard to stay hopeful?

Think of your support system, how does it differ from the young people's experiences you've read?

How have you reacted when someone has opened up about their mental health? Or if you've told someone of an illness that has affected you, what helped and what didn't?

How can you build an environment that supports mental and physical health equally? What changes can you make to the way you work?

Key takeaways…

- Take time to get to know me, if you don't have time, fight for it!

- Listen to me to understand me not to answer or plan for me.

- If we both understand each other, I will have a better chance of understanding why you make the decisions and recommendations you do.

- Support us to live through Covid and other global challenges that lie ahead.

Chapter 5

Our experiences of being understood and its impact

- For good
- On solid ground
- Too young to understand
- What to pack
- A big blur of words
- She can and she did
- We can change our minds

For good

There was often a person from social services or the family court at our placement. They came to ask questions, usually at the same time, or to tell us what was happening. It could be the social worker, or the independent reviewing officer, or even the solicitor. Today it was our guardian.

Our guardian is kind. She's our favourite out of the official sounding people. She always listens to us and tries her best to get our voices heard in court. Plus, she always bought us sweets, which was an obvious bonus.

Today it seemed different. Our carers were smiling and happy but did not drop hints as to why they were so excited. It was probably something we would find out after our little meeting, so we didn't read much into it.

"Maggie has something to tell you!" Our carer announced as we sat down on the floor, looking up expectantly. Our first thought was that it was another thing about court. Much of it didn't make sense as were only seven and eight years old.

We chatted about what we'd been up to and how we were, then she dropped the bomb. What was said exactly neither of us can remember but we know that afterwards, there was an eruption of joy and happy tears. The announcement was that we would be staying with our carers in a long-term placement – for the rest of our childhood.

"Oh no! We are stuck with you for another 10 years!" Our carers laughed affectionately as we danced around the living room, giddy with happiness at the amazing news.

Anonymous

Our message to professionals: Be your best self when you're with us. It increases trust and shows you care. A little bit of inspiration goes a long way.

On solid ground

I started to feel really different from my friends when the summer holidays came. Everyone was talking about meeting their family and going on holiday, but I had no access to my passport so I couldn't leave the country.

I was very young when the court case started and only knew my parents weren't together. My friends at school didn't have to worry about being separated from their brother or their mum. Some days I dreaded going home from school in case they were gone when I got there. A constant worry overshadowed everything: that I would have to go back and live with my father. That made it harder for me to enjoy things with my family. I would wonder if it would be the last time.

Sometimes I would have to miss going to my friend's house because a professional would come to talk with us. I'm sure my friends knew something was happening, but I didn't fully know what was happening myself, so how could I explain it to anyone else?

I was only able to talk about my worries to my family. The court case separated me from my friends. It was a huge part of my life that no-one else understood.

The professional people were good, they were nice and listened when I told them how I felt and what I wanted. But they never properly explained what I wanted to know. I was always halfway in the dark. It made the ground beneath my feet unsteady. I couldn't relax and feel completely safe because nothing felt solid.

Being different from my friends and being uncertain about my future were the worst parts of the experience. If what was happening had been properly explained to me, in terms I understood, not spoken over my head, I think my life would have been much less stressful and I wouldn't have felt like I was living in limbo while my parents divorced.

Now I live with my mum and siblings and we are happy. We have the freedom to go wherever we want to because we have passports and there is no need to feel left out or different. My life makes sense.

Anonymous

Our message to professionals: Understanding exactly what's happening can make difficult periods easier for us.

Too young to understand

I wasn't even given the chance to say goodbye, it all happened so fast. My siblings were shouting, wailing, my mum was crying. People were in our house, giving orders, taking pictures.

"Go pack your things, enough for a few days."

I tried, but I had no idea what was going on. In a flurry of noise and activity I was bustled into a big car and driven away. I clung to my bag, haphazardly stuffed, for comfort. I'd never had to pack a bag before. It was a little Dora the Explorer suitcase; my sister and I had kept dolls' clothes in it. We drove for a long time, nowhere I recognised, past streets and streets of houses I'd never seen. I gulped back tears.

I was delivered to strangers, led through a strange house, and settled in a plain white bedroom. I was seven and nothing made sense. I wished I'd packed more. I hadn't even brought a stuffed teddy, or my favourite toy to play with. Just my Dora the Explorer suitcase and I didn't have that for long. My first foster carer took it from me and gave it to their niece. That was the last thing I had from home.

In the days that followed, my older siblings were allowed to see my mum, but I wasn't. Was it all my fault? I must have done something wrong. She didn't like me. She didn't want me. I couldn't work out why else she wouldn't want to speak to me. I kept asking my social worker questions:

"Why am I here?"
"When will I see my mum?"
"When can I go home?"
"What's going on?"

I never got an answer. She made me feel like I was being stupid for trying to understand.

Eventually I stopped asking.

The people I stayed with were kind, but I drew away, closed myself up. I began to struggle with forming attachments and accepting love. If even my mum didn't want me, who would?

When I was seven, my siblings and I were taken away from our mother. I never saw her again. I was placed with strangers, given no explanation or assurance. I was considered too young to see her, and too young to understand. As a child, I could only assume I had done something wrong, and that belief, however misguided, has stayed with me ever since.

Anonymous

Our message to professionals: I need to understand what's happening to me, or your intervention might do more harm than good.

What to pack

When you hear a professional saying, "Go pack your bags for a few days," it can be stressful and hard to think about what you need. Most people reading this won't be in the same situation, but just in case I have done a list. From my experience these are the top 10 things I think can't be forgotten.

Grab your suitcase or rucksack and find:

1. 7 tops
2. 7 trousers
3. Enough pants and socks for the time being
4. Stuff teddy in for comfort as it can be scary
5. 4 pairs pj's
6. Books
7. Chargers
8. iPad, phones, computers
9. A blanket
10. And grab your top five favourite toys

Better to take your favourite things when you have the chance, than to miss out like I did. Make sure you say all the goodbyes you need to. Don't worry about toiletries, toothpaste or shampoo. The foster carers you are going to will have some ready. Take things from your childhood. I didn't pack any of my toys, since I thought I would be coming back. Every day I wish I'd packed more, so I hope this helps anyone, even just one person who is reading this.

Anonymous

Our message to professionals: These moments are critical. Help me not to have regrets. I am a child, as important as any other. When children are moving, help them to know what to pack and do this with deep respect and care for the trauma we are experiencing.

A big blur of words

Everywhere is a big blur of sound. I feel dizzy with all the loud noises in the atmosphere. My small words are useless. People are talking and talking. Whatever I say, there's no impact. I try to shout, "Stop!" But no one listens. The colour that comes to mind is red. Redness everywhere.

I remember being so stressed that sometimes I would scream, sometimes just go quiet. I had to overcome the stress of my words making no impact and feeling useless. Most of the time I had to go with what I was meant to do and not what I wanted to do.

I wasn't told a lot about what was going on, but I knew we had to move country for a reason. I was three years old at the time.

Now that I'm older, I realise that's why communication was so tough. I understand we moved countries to be safer and I am very glad about the decision that my mum made.

After six years, there are no more court cases and I can stay with my mum. She listens to my opinions and considers them in any decisions made. I was grateful for the Cafcass professionals who came to my house as I could tell them truthfully how I felt, and I knew it would have an impact on the court decision.

I feel comfortable with no more shouting. I can speak when I am asked to and I am listened to as well, which I couldn't be happier about.

Anonymous

Our message to professionals: Young children may need help to communicate, but we understand more than you think.

She can and she did

Sometimes I ask myself how things would have turned out if I hadn't gone into those woods. I held his hand. He let me paddle in the river and told me stories from his childhood. He put his arms round me to dry me off. I remember asking him when I could go back to Mummy and he grabbed me so tightly I couldn't pull myself free. There was a knife at my neck and I was forced to the ground. He was lying on top of me, his breathing getting heavier. The rest remains one big blur of his face and body and then running.

It was as if I had frozen in time but everything around me still carried on. People were growing up, moving away, but a part of me was still trapped in that evening. My mum let me believe that I was just dreaming. She said my nightmare would end soon. Yet it never did. Years went by. Every day tore away another chunk of my identity to the point I was a stranger to myself.

This is why I'm writing to you, the professionals. You denied me the chance to experience a childhood despite me physically begging you to take me away from my mum and dad. You came to my house and sat next to the man who raped me and believed him. Why? Because you thought he was my father, that as the adult he knew best.

Six years later, the man is arrested and then you say to me, "If only I had known." You accused me of having a vivid fantasy. Only when the man is in handcuffs did you believe me. I want to know why you didn't ask more questions?

I found out later that the man isn't my real father. I don't know which is worse – to be abused by a stranger or your own flesh and blood. But I can tell you one thing: I want justice.

I am strong, I know what I want.

Fortunately, one single woman believed me: my therapist. Without her I would not have made it. It only took one person to change my life, to give me hope. Now I am loved and cared for, my trauma is getting less and less. I believe in myself and can forgive you.

I said I would be free and now in four weeks I am getting on a train alone and will start my next chapter overseas.

Anonymous

A letter to professionals dealing with my case – dated 16th July 2021.

We can change our minds

Age 6
I am asked if I want to see my dad. I am unsure. "In between" I say.
I stay in contact.

Age 13
I am sat with my mum at the table. She is listening to me and writing down what I'm saying.

I want
To live a happy and successful life.
To be an engineer.
To help others.

I don't want
To be afraid.
To be abusive, manipulative, controlling.
To be like my dad.

It was hard to cut off parts of my life, like my Xbox groups and my old room. I know myself and what I want. I know that not seeing my dad is best for me.

I wonder what he is doing, but I am happier now.

Anonymous

Our message to professionals: As we grow up, our opinions change, that should be ok.

> You can find a happier place, we did

...rsevere, your voice will be heard - even if it doesn't happen straight away

Seeing others going through similar experiences opened my eyes and gave me courage, you can get through this

If you aren't open about things no-one will know what you feel, they can't read your mind

's ok to be confused

For professionals

What do the stories in this chapter suggest about the way you work with children and young people? What impacts on the quality of your listening?

Think back to your own childhood. Do you remember a situation where nothing made sense? What would have helped?

Have you ever been misunderstood, ignored, or dismissed? How did it make you feel? Did it stop you from speaking out in the future?

What's your recipe for improving your understanding? Reflect on the way you listen and the influence on the actions you then take?

What's your relationship with feedback? How open are you to hearing and engaging with feedback from others? What do you do with it when you hear it?

How could you be more creative and courageous in your work to support children in the family justice system.

Key takeaways…

- Look for evidence, ask questions, listen actively to what's said and what isn't.

- Check we understand what's happening or your intervention might do more harm than good.

- Be your best self when you're with us, it increases trust and shows you care.

- Walk in our shoes so that you can empathise with our experiences and therefore understand our wishes and feelings better.

Chapter 6

Next steps

- Postscript
- Mind your language
- Resources
- More about FJYPB and Cafcass
- Glossary

Postscript

Having got to the end of the book, you will now have – if you didn't already – a true sense of the bravery and courage shown by children, and the very complex situations in which they can find themselves. Children keep on giving. They continue to trust adults despite the many who have let them down. We have to use these stories to move the family justice system forward, guided by the specific calls to action that you will have seen at the end of each story and the reflections you have made as you have moved through the book.

At Cafcass, among our priorities are improving our practice so that children and their families understand our reasoning for the recommendations we make, taking their feedback about their experiences with us so that we learn what we have done well, and what we need to do differently. We are focusing on developing trusting relationships so that it is easier for children to share with a stranger – a person who has authority to profoundly influence their futures – what life is like.

We want to continue holding them at the centre of all we do and, in sponsoring this book, Cafcass hopes to inspire change in our organisation and also in the wider children's justice and social care systems. The young people are clear about what they want to see happen and the difference it will make to others who find themselves in family justice proceedings.

All of them show great potential through these pieces and in their many contributions to the work of the Board, the government, and the family courts – all made while they are busy becoming their future selves. We are proud to know and work alongside them. The call to action is made. Now it is for us to lead and to change in response to walking in their shoes.

Jacky Tiotto
Chief Executive, Cafcass

Mind your language

Here's a list of words and phrases that we often hear during family law proceedings. We want to encourage all professionals to stop using these and to think about the ways in which they speak to children and young people and how they refer to us in their reports, on file, and to other professionals.

I am not a subject child or an object.

I would like to be referred to by my name. The proceedings are about my life. The only thing worse than being referred to as a subject child is a non-subject child. Please think about how you talk about the people involved in family law proceedings.

Me and my family are not service users.

This sounds too formal and unconnected. We are a family, and I am a child.

I am not a CASE or a number.

I am a person, so please don't talk about how many cases you have or about your case plan. Talk about how many children and young people you are helping.

A connected child

usually refers to my brothers or sisters. They are not connected. They are my family. Also don't use the word SIBLINGS. Say brothers and sisters because this is how I refer to them.

Looked After Child (LAC).

This makes me feel patronised and as though I am different. I am a child like any other. Please don't label me.

I am not a problem or a problem child, but I may be faced with problems and challenges that make me react in a way that is difficult to others. Think about how the label 'problem child' will affect me.

Beyond parental control.
This is very upsetting to hear and to read about. It makes me feel that I have no hope or that there is no way to change or make things better. Think about how you describe me. What will I think about myself in later years if I read this?

I do not have behaviour issues, but rather you have observed some aspect to the way I respond to things that can be challenging. Write or talk about what you have observed and the possible causes. Put yourself in my shoes. How would you react? Is my reaction a fair response to my situation?

Access and contact suggests that I need permission.
Who gives the permission? What happens if they say no? Also, what are my rights? Instead, talk or write about me 'spending time with' a member of my family.

Orders: Child Arrangements Orders; Prohibited Steps Orders; Secure Order and other court terminology is very confusing. I may not understand what an order is or what it means. Talk to me and make sure I understand what decisions have been made about my life and write clearly about them in my file and how it will affect me. Also, 16.4s, S7, S31 etc. What do these numbers mean to me?

CIAF, ISO, ICO, CYP

Any sort of acronyms in my notes are confusing. I am not sure what they mean, and I don't understand how they are important to me. Write or say them in full and give me an explanation.

My diversity is part of me and it allows me to express who I am and the things that are important to me. I want you to talk to me and explore my diversity. Talk and write about my diversity in the way I have described it to you. Do not write on my file or on report, no 'diversity issues'.

Kids. We are not goats, but children and young people. Think about how you use the word 'kid(s)'. It can feel patronising.

My wishes and feelings are not fantasy but rather my hopes for my future. So please don't talk about or write about me as if I live in a fantasy world.

Rather than talk or write about my **split family** because this feels negative, or a blended family as this can feel confusing, just explain what this means for me.

I will want to know when I can spend time with my parents/carers and family members. The term **shared care** feels strange and as though I need 'care'. Just explain to me when I spend time with my family.

It is really common to talk about court hearings with their titles or acronyms such as: **FHDRA, DRA**, and **IRH**. I do not know what these are, why they need to take place, who will be there, or what the possible outcomes may be. Please think about this when talking to me. Make sure I understand what a court hearing is, what the outcome is likely to be, and how this will affect me.

Please remember these tips when you speak to me, about me or write about me. AND correct others if they don't consider the language that they use.

— Our top tips for professionals —

We have developed a range of top tips aimed at professionals working with children and young people. You can find our top tips posters and short films at:
www.cafcass.gov.uk/family-justice-young-peoples-board/

There are resources on:
- Top tips for respecting children and young people's diversity, disabilities, autism, transgender and LGB

- Top tips for Cafcass practitioners, social workers, teachers, and judges who work with children and young people while they are in the family justice system

- Check our guidance for separating parents and for brothers and sisters

- We have tips for supporting children and young people affected by domestic abuse and mental health issues. Plus there's our guidance on spending time together online.

Voice of the Child conference
The annual Voice of the Child conference is completely led, organised, and run by members of the FJYPB, attracting an audience of about 200 delegates, including senior figures and family justice professionals.

Our goal is to bring together the key professionals in the family justice world to deliver speeches, participate in panel discussions and lead workshops that are ideas-focused and on a wide range of key family justice topics. The conference also provides the opportunity to interact with and learn from Board members and fellow attendees to discuss how to implement best practice when working with children and young people. Find out more on our webpage.

And...

There are also a wider range of resources for professionals on the main Cafcass website aimed at judges, magistrates and local authorities and covering legislation, research and policies. For any professional working directly with children, there are many tools including: a My Needs, Wishes and Feelings Pack; a Child Impact Tool; and a My Family Court Record resource.

More about the FJYPB

The Family Justice Young People's Board (FJYPB) are a group of more than 70 children and young people aged between eight and 25 years old, who live across England and Wales. All our members have either had direct experience of the family justice system or have an interest in children's rights and the family courts.

Our overall aim is to support the work of the Family Justice Board, which aims to deliver improvements to the family justice system so that it provides the best result for children who come into contact with it.

We work hard to help ensure that the work of the Family Justice Board is child-centred and child-inclusive. We do this by participating in all its meetings to enable young people to have a direct say in its work. In doing this, we work closely with other young people's groups and stakeholders within family justice.

We work to promote the voice of children and young people that experience family breakdown, including those children and young people who are involved in family court proceedings. We do this by actively taking part in various meetings, projects and events, and working together with various agencies and organisations.

Who we work with – The FJYPB works with a range of family justice organisations and agencies. These include, but are not limited to:
- Cafcass
- Ministry of Justice

- Family Justice Board
- Mediation services (including National Family Mediation, NFM)
- National Association of Child Contact Centres (NACCC)
- HM Courts and Tribunals Service
- Judiciary
- Local authorities

If you are new to Cafcass...

Cafcass represents children in family court cases in England. We independently advise the family courts about what is safe for children and in their best interests. We put their needs, wishes and feelings first, making sure that children's voices are heard at the heart of the family court setting. Operating within the law set by Parliament (Criminal Justice and Court Services Act 2000) and under the rules and directions of the family courts, we are independent of the courts, social services, education and health authorities and all similar agencies.

Our duty is to safeguard and promote the welfare of children going through the family justice system, supporting over 140,000 children every year by understanding their experiences and speaking up for them when the family court makes critical decisions about their futures.

Cafcass is the largest employer of qualified social workers in England and is deeply committed to making a positive difference to each child we support. We are proud that everyone working for Cafcass is united in improving the lives of children, families, and carers.

Our duty is to safeguard and promote the welfare of children going through the family justice system. Our experienced Family Court Advisers may be asked by the court to work with families and then advise the court on what we consider to be the best interests of the children involved in three main areas:
- divorce and separation, sometimes called 'private law', where parents or carers can't agree on arrangements for their children

- care proceedings, sometimes called 'public law', where social services have serious concerns about the safety or welfare of a child
- adoption, which can be either public or private law.

We also actively work with our partners to identify solutions to help reduce the increasing pressures on the family courts and to improve the experiences and outcomes for children and families.

https://www.cafcass.gov.uk/about-cafcass/

Glossary

This glossary covers terms related to the experiences in this book. A more extensive list of terms related to family justice proceedings can be found at www.cafcass.org.uk

Children and Family Court Advisory and Support Service (Cafcass) – This is an organisation which works with children and young people and their families, and then advises the family court on what it considers to be in the best interests of each child.

Cafcass worker – Depending on what the family court has ordered Cafcass to do, the Cafcass worker is sometimes known as a practitioner or officer, they can also be known as a Family Court Adviser or a Children's Guardian (these titles are used in the pieces in this book) see below for more detail.

Care order – An order made by the family court when the local authority can prove that a child or young person living in their area is not being looked after properly.

Child arrangements order – When people can't agree on where a child might live or who they should see, the family court might be asked to decide. The judge will look at what is best for the child or young person and make a decision setting out what people must do.

Children's guardian – Sometimes when the problems within a family are really difficult then the family court will ask for a children's guardian to help them. The children's guardian is an independent person who is there to keep the court focused on what is best for the child or young person. They will also appoint a solicitor to act for the young person in court.

Family court – This is where important decisions are made about children, young people, and their families. It is different to criminal courts where people go when they might have done something wrong. Decisions in the family court are made by judges or magistrates when people can't agree about what is best for a child or young person.

Family Court Adviser (FCA) – Sometimes the family court may ask an FCA to meet with a child or young people to talk about their wishes and feelings and to make sure the family court hears what they have to say. The FCA also gives their view to the court about what is best for the child. FCAs do not need to meet all children and young people because sometimes families can agree themselves on what is best.

Foster carer – People who give a home to children and young people who need a safe place to live. They may have children of their own, or other foster children living with them, in which case you would all live in the same house together.

Judge – Sometimes families have problems which they might find too hard to sort out by themselves. A judge works in a family court, listens to everybody, and then decides what is best for the child or young person involved in the case. They have the final say and will make the decision about that child or young person's life.

Legal Adviser – A legally qualified person who helps magistrates in the family court apply the law. They do not play any part in the decision-making process but are there to advise.

Local authority or local council (also known as children's social care or social services) – This organisation is responsible for making sure all children and young people in their local area are kept safe by the people who care for them.

Placement order – An order which allows the local authority to place a child with suitable adopters following care proceedings (even if the parents do not agree).

Private law – These cases are brought to the family court by private individuals, generally in connection with divorce or parents' separation. The family court may make a child arrangements order, prohibited steps order or a specific issues order or no order at all.

Public law – Public law cases are brought to the family court by local authorities where they are worried that a child or young person is not being looked after safely. The family court may make a care order, a supervision order, or no order at all.

Social worker – These specially trained people help to make sure children and young people are safe and properly looked after. They will work with families to help make it possible for children to stay safely with them. If the family court decides that it is not possible, they will help to make sure there is somewhere else that is safe where a child can live.

Solicitor – A legally trained person who provides advice to people going through the family court and can speak for them in court.

Supervision order – A supervision order makes the local authority take responsibility for advising, assisting, and befriending a young person, and ensuring that the child or young person is kept safe in the care of their parents.

Thank you!

...urt staff, solicitors, mediators, barristers, legal secretaries, and advisors, key workers, local council workers, cass staff and managers, judges, social workers, contact centres, teachers, carers, magistrates, police, and everyone who works in family justice!

From the FJYPB

for reading this book and keeping us safe. We know your work doesn't always get the recognition it deserves, we notice the hard work you put in and it makes a massive difference to our lives.

About Shared Press

Stories that Matter
Cafcass has worked with Dawn Reeves of Shared Press on this project. Shared Press is an independent publisher and social enterprise with a remit to share stories that engage with the sharp edges and messy boundaries of modern life, give voice to new writers who care about ideas and innovation and inspire new creative conversations with readers. We focus on public life and public services.

About Dawn Reeves – Director
Dawn is a story activist, creative facilitator, public services expert, and writer. A former director in a large public sector organisation, she now works with a range of clients looking for creative approaches to making change happen. Her energy and enthusiasm for this work come from a deep curiosity about the world and a drive to collaborate. She's a published novelist, has written for the Guardian and was the writer-in-residence at the Chartered Institute for Public Finance and Accountancy (CIPFA).

Contact her via dawn@sharedpress.co.uk

More from Shared Press

It's a small list, but it's perfectly formed and it's growing…

Our futures now – Barnsley 2030 (December 2021)

One story – Councils, covid and better futures (March 2021)

Leading change, inspiring learners – for London South-East Education Group (October 2020)

We've got this – Art, ethics, and public service (November 2019)

Getting to the heart of it – Transforming services for children in Bexley (March 2019)

Town Hall – buildings, people, and power (December 2018)

Boldly and Rightly – Public Service in Bexley (June 2018)

We Know What We Are – Thriller (November 2017)

Holding Up the Mirror – True stories of public service in a post-truth world (October 2017)

Under the skin: Stories about the culture of place for Grant Thornton LLP (October 2016)

Walk Tall – Being a 21st century public servant (May 2016)

Making Our Mark – A story collection for Greenwich University (June 2015 plus global edition June 2016)

Change the Ending – Flash fiction (September 2014)

Hard Change – Thriller (March 2013)

For more information see www.sharedpress.co.uk

Lightning Source UK Ltd.
Milton Keynes UK
UKHW050801040222
398186UK00001B/24